In *Sexting Ghosts*, Joanna Valente invites us to join them in their haunted psychiatrist's chair for a cinematic Q&A with the ghosts and gods of the future past. These poems together form an epic flush with oblique strategies for survival. Valente's arguments sear then soften, become inquiries, persistent efforts to either understand or to cut ties with what time has shed. Ghosts and humans alike know the exhausting experience of being a human trapped in a body. Ghosts, too, are jailed in their forms: "Ghosts of the dead / crowd a clear / prism" in Valente's New York City; they crowd the internet, subway platforms, memories and poems, where Valente faithfully returns to exorcise their gorgeous lan-guage, "noticing every detail as if each / matters as much as Da Vinci's ear." With rage clear as daylight, Valente chants, "All of your heroes are dead," reminding us that egos and acts and bodies are transient, while reassuring us "It was just you & I & / it was a beautiful snow globe" — each beautiful thing, when they write it, becomes a spirit trapped in its page, reaching out to be read and cherished for its mystery. —**Jasmine Dreame Wagner**, author of *On a Clear Day* and *Rings*

Much in the way that Anne Carson uses Geryon as a siphon of contemporary sexual politics, so too does Joanna C. Valente channel their prowess through myth-making. Whether their mythos is familial, elemental, and/or technological, their poetry falls uneasily into those writ traditions. A poetry jagged and strange, Valente unearths the clumsy and mortified gods responsible for mortal violence and whim; personifies family members in order to queer and estrange their bonds; and reconciles their body against the machinery of the gaze. In my favorite poem, they ask, "how do you eat pizza & make it / art   how do you hang // flags and make it true." Their relentless confrontation with the physical finds them inconsolably digital when they suppose, "Maybe everything / is simply an illusion." Here is a poetry inside the nexus of past, present, and future, whose "only dream is a bodiless hand / stroking a child," who knows "there is no home in america / for us." **—Natalie Eilbert**, author of *Indictus*

SEXTING GHOSTS

JOANNA C. VALENTE

UNKNOWN PRESS

Published by UNKNOWN PRESS
Copyright © 2018 by Joanna C. Valente
All rights reserved

Edited by Devin Kelly
Cover art and design by Ted Chevalier
Interior layout by Bud Smith

CONTENTS

I. HUMANS

Daughter 13
Brother 14
Son 15
Mother 16
Father 17
Sister 18
Wife 19
Husband 21
Grandmother 22
Grandfather 23
Stepfather 24
Stepsister 25
Stepmother 26
Cousin 27
Mother-in-law 28

II. HEAVEN/HELL, AKA: THE INTERNET

Everyone is an Asshole   31
Everyone Hates Everyone   32
No One Ever Really Leaves You   33
Love in the Age of the Internet   34
No One Likes You Until You're Dead   35
When Blue Becomes Magenta   36
I Am Home Alone On Friday Night Because No One Loves Me   37
That Time You Were Drunk and Went To a Tarot Card Reader and Tried To Kiss Her and Instead She Told You To Leave   39
There is a Man & a Woman   41
Coney Island Baby   42
You Are the Universe   43
Unable to Have Children   45
I Have Become Uninteresting   46
A Tale of Two Worlds   48
Why is Everything Terrible   50
The End of the World Happened on the Internet   51
The House No One Lives In   52

III. GODS

God of Corn Video Chats With God of Trees   57
Good of Internet   59
God of Metal   60
God of Light Meets Good of Water   61
God of Destruction   62
There is no Dana, Only Zuul   64
God of the MTA   66
God of Parables Says Murder Me, You Sweet Daring   67
God of Hunger and God of Sanitation Go on a Date   68
God of Hunger's One Night Stand   69
God of Rain Watches Porn   70
Planets Rotate, Red & Erect   71
God of Sound Talks After a Hiatus   72
God of Punishment Hears Their Last Words   74
God of Thunder Divorces God of Lightning   75
God of Water   77
God of Air   78
Good of Loneliness   79
God og Gravity   80
The Waters Belong to Us   81
Humans Don't Know You   82

For my dead, my ghosts, and you

I. HUMAN

DAUGHTER

How long did it take you to get here?

I'd like to cash my days in now

When was the first time you made love?

Man holds gun to my stomach

What will you say to your children?

I say take it, there's so much for you
to take

What have you lost?

The moon has a red glare
encircling my legs

I haven't been able to move
for 5 yrs

Who do you miss most?

Red tentacles killing flies
between my legs

gulping salt to sleep on water
see brother cover my face in purple

Would you have anyone killed?

It has been years

BROTHER

What are you listening to?

Men moaning in their sleep—dreaming in cunt dimensions

Who was the first person to hit you?

TV's blare from heaven

When did you stop praying?

Before my childhood began to smell of dead roaches
& fractured skulls

What do you remember most of your childhood?

When sister told me if I masturbated my fingers
will burn until ash is gone from ash—said she'd take me

to CBGB's but then I found out CBGB's died w/ punk

How do you want to be remembered?

As a deer heart being held from yr chest
watching it squirm as it loses oxygen

& beats slow hum to white noise as radios
repeat yr body is full to the brim w/ shit

SON

When did you first experience death?

At home, I eat dinner
alone in the bathroom

Describe your body

Two people loved each other
at the same time once

When did your body start changing?

I don't know if it exists
b/c I only saw it on the internet

How long does it take you to get to work in the morning?

A woman asked me if the R goes
to the Atlantic Ocean

I kissed her outside a gay bar
told her to spread eagle

said this is how full of shit
you are

How old are you?

Don't respect the organ that keeps
me alive

MOTHER

Who was your first love?

My only dream is a bodiless hand
stroking a child, canyon for a face

Have you seen the dead?

We are a carriage of hummingbirds

When did you become a mother?

On the Q, a boy took a feather out
of his mother's coat, put it in the palm
of her hand

When did you stop believing in God?

Make 12 an hour, chalk it up
to life experience

FATHER

When was the last time you saw your mother?

Do the dead materialize

What did your father teach you?

Death is everywhere else, my body
isn't everywhere else

What is your profession?

Missing subway tiles

How do you dream?

I read Craig's List ads for sugar daddies

When did you first love someone?

All that I want is already in me

When did you first lose someone?

All that I want is already in me

SISTER

Are you male or female?

Dream song

What did you eat for breakfast?

Hands of Polish grandmothers

What time did you go to bed?

Witching hour

Tell me of your suffering

Men have always tried to touch me

What do you see?

A man with a blue face kisses me
until he isn't blue anymore

It has been timed perfectly by the gods
Wind is most fierce around his face

Where do you live?

My shit is yr shit

How do you want to die?

On a mattress of air, no one around
to touch

WIFE

Where were you born?

Standing in the women's
bathroom at Otto's Shrunken Head

hoping to god I'm not pregnant
hoping to a god I'm not

pregnant a second time, second
baby death, last time abortion

How did I let my body do this

Why can't I let my body do what I
want it to do

When did you start bleeding?

Solar debris fell to New York
from Jupiter & I was watching

Eraserhead at Sunshine
& the guy sitting next to me kept

saying it's okay
to no one

What was the last thing you said to your mother?

My mother told me I lost faith
in god after I was raped

I said, wouldn't you

Who are you in love with?

I still think of him when I listen
to The Ronettes

when my ears pop
on the subway, my body jerking

& his body breaking
into mine like ice cubes

in boiling water--but no one
can ruin The Ronettes

for me, not even him
not even me

HUSBAND

When was the first time you recognized yourself in a mirror?

I slept in her bedroom
at her dad's apt in Port Chester

we didn't even bother to quiet
during sex

Do you make direct eye contact during intercourse?

The "I" is imminent

What is your favorite meal?

Everything dead eats itself
I want to eat something alive

Would you consider yourself a free spirit?

On the subway, I get out
my keys before my stop

Do you miss your childhood?

Don't you wish a brick
would fall from the sky

What do you love about your wife?

In bed her belly spills
out onto mine, a rail yard

where subways go
to die

She dreams about places
that are nowhere

GRANDMOTHER

When were you born?

Ford built houses
for people to live in
if they worked

All of my children
were born in
the same house

When did you move to Brooklyn?

I got caught
in a rainstorm

Every cab rode past
me, so I gave one

the finger and he
thought I hailed him over

What do you love about your body?

The search for the other
for an alternate

whether it's a person
or time

specifically molded
just for me

doesn't matter which;
it's the thirst

for water

GRANDFATHER

What do you want to do before you die?

Cram a violin neck into the neck
of a man to get an honest sound

Describe a usual day

I am shrinking while this tiny ball
grows another liver inside my lungs

How did you become comfortable around others?

When I'm standing close to another
human, I feel awkward so I usually act
more awkward to counter-balance it

Who was your first love?

I never met a woman whose entire body
wasn't made from Revlon

What are you missing?

A nerve connecting two hearts;
I left my wife by putting a note

on her pillow saying be back in five
I was never back

STEPFATHER

What was your first language?

Riding elevators to the top floor
yearning for horizontal movement

What did your father teach you about manhood?

Eating flesh with a bone knife, how to sharpen
the knife until the marrow disappeared
in another's blood—usually my blood

What do you remember of your mother?

At night she left the house, slept
all morning in black lace and tarred skin.

Her body bloated and purplish
when I found her on the kitchen floor

How do you spend your free time?

Gutting fish listening to Long Island
talk because I've stopped

having anything to say, it's
just sound now

STEPSISTER

When did you lose your virginity?

At one point being
alone scared me.
Now my legs open
for the thought.

How is your relationship with your father?

I have switched
cities seven times.

Where is your blood?

We are in a bathtub
as big as a football
stadium and we are
ashamed of giving life

so we hide our
blood in towels.

How did you become human?

Sometimes I ask Father
to press from
behind me so I
can feel how he
survived.

STEPMOTHER

What do you own?

The world is between
my legs

When are you happy?

Who I am when
I am not myself

Why did you marry?

Why would anyone jog on
this road?

It's asking to die

What has aged you?

Everyone reciting someone
Else's wedding vows—

Do you hate Mondays?

Give me your tired
Give me your poor

Describe your twenties.

Parties celebrating watered
Down versions of god

COUSIN

Where were you born?

A mouth full of hot coal
sometimes mistaken
as god in a mother's body
as a lamb's belly

When did you stop believing your mother?

Riding the subway while
a man ate his own flesh
in pieces like sirloin

Do you fall in love easily?

A woman's breast contains
milky suns and rain-filled stars
because women are the
butter knife in a house empty

of bread. I crave rye toast
even when my mouth bleeds.

MOTHER-IN-LAW

Describe adulthood

Most things mean nothing

What is your favorite time of day?

A separate reality
coming into being
silverish & freezing
as a foul abandoned
by it's mother & tasting
fresh cherries for the
first time

Have you seen the dead?

What can't the body do?

What was the first word you spoke?

A shed in the woods holds
roots deep as the sky
but not the heart

Sometimes ghosts eat the hands
of the living
covering their tongues
in decadent moonlike mystery
masked as worship

II. HEAVEN/HELL, AKA: THE INTERNET

EVERYONE IS AN ASSHOLE

She was standing alone.
Above the grates a sound

like water falling
onto ground

and people walking in the rain
as if they don't exist
inside themselves

bumping their umbrellas
into each other as if other bodies
don't exist.

As if it doesn't matter
that other people exist.

And maybe they're right
in thinking that, maybe nothing
matters.

Maybe everything
is simply an illusion

or maybe we're just conditioned
to being assholes

use falling
water as an excuse.

The train door opens & she slips
inside, sits down & stares

into her phone,
talking to no one.

EVERYONE HATES EVERYONE

I didn't pick up
when you called me that night
because I thought you were drunk

and butt-dialed me at a funeral
for someone you don't even
know and my body was in

another state watching
a man undress and there was nothing
uglier than when he

unzipped his pants than
a crocodile and what is the one
thing so beautiful you can't

bear to look away but you can't
possess and you'll drive
home after hours of hands

shaking your hand and condolences
for someone who would probably
hate you and there is that mirror.

NO ONE EVER REALLY LEAVES YOU

I am dead.
I meet a woman
who is not a girl.
In the sky, she sees
a phantom

who has our face.
It looks like us.

*

All of the birds have died
There are no birds
left in Philly.

Every light has been eaten
by things called demons.
I am not afraid of them.

They shines back as a constellation
w/out stars—

an immense stone bath, a reverse vagina
trampled inward.

LOVE IN THE AGE OF THE INTERNET

A diamond bullet tears
my teeth out

while our mother
swims in a glass jar

her fins vulnerable like legs
her mouth is a skeleton

of our house
now gone

is the garage full
of paper mâché masks

a failed American Dream

that loves time so much
it mimics a Roman fall.

NO ONE LIKES YOU UNTIL YOU'RE DEAD

In Coney Island, there is a body
who thinks he is a god stranded
on uneven sand making love
to earth in polluted space.

A woman's hands smell like plastic
suntan lotion bottles. Swarms of
moths stroke her back, wings

whirring like a smile. Why bother
when the cancer's already there?

She swats them with her plastic
Chinese fan from the corner 99 cent
store, thinking about the hands

who make dollar store dreams.

WHEN BLUE BECOMES MAGENTA

Ghosts of the dead
crowd a clear
prism like biting
into nectarines and
tasting putrid twilight,
lost in the purposeless of
lines in a body bag.

A sext is sent—
no one answers.

I AM HOME ALONE ON A FRIDAY NIGHT BECAUSE NO ONE LOVES ME

text message 11:03 pm:
someone is watching me,
i spilled my gin inside my thighs

& pretend to sext a guy i met
on tinder

text message 11:05 pm:
does his face look like punched leather
or thin as guitar strings?

pics or it didn't happen

text message 11:11 pm:
he told me to make a wish
for the world to end before midnight

i wonder if he thinks of me before he takes a shit,
if inside me feels like water boiling,
a mosh
pit of sting rays

text message 11:35 pm:
dead men are the only men
who listen

text message 11:37 pm:
that must be why i'm in
buffering hell

text message 11:55 pm:
come over? let me know when
yr body is no longer
in yr house & no longer yrs
but someone else's

THAT TIME YOU WERE DRUNK AND WENT TO A TAROT READER AND TRIED TO KISS HER AND INSTEAD SHE TOLD YOU TO LEAVE

Your mother talked to you as a kid about loneliness because she was lonely and had always been lonely just like you are alone on the train smelling perfume samples as a way to bring back all the women that are no longer women but memories that make you feel lonely before you fall

asleep at night and it finally hits you like a baseball to the head: your mother was right when she said there's something comfortable about the idea that we become invisible as we age—unfuckable, so therefore, unthinkable and she's right: you're only interested in other people when you know there's a possibility that both of your bodies might fuck each other

like cars passing outside your bedroom window swimming in a mechanical ocean that isn't dangerous where no one drowns but everyone is already dead and goddamn happy about it because no one's afraid anymore and here you are still so afraid of being alone after you've died

and there's no way to kill yourself so you do the only thing you know how to do: you try to make love with the first woman you see but not even she wants to deal with your bullshit and your mother stopped talking to you once you turned eighteen and your new mother's name is gin but she drowns you every night and you see nothing but black and a man hanging from a tree

THERE IS A MAN & A WOMAN

There is a man in Brooklyn
who can't remember his dreams
so when he tells a woman

he'll dream of her, her only body
hushes like stained glass gutting
fish into a cherry blossom

separated into thunderous
threads sewn inside his spleen
into a thistle crown now

the hands of two elk-faced
angels spilling medieval suns
through their mouths as if to sing

holy, holy, holy backwards
pixelated by data reverberation
against the stars still

alive just as the pulse
inside the man inside the woman
coarsely dissolving

in a metallic gleam beyond
the Verrazano drowning the rest
of the world in defiance

before dawn, unalone
as the man & woman, a question
of dreams or eyes.

CONEY ISLAND BABY

In Wellfleet, there are waves
with your name pushing & pulling

me in like thirsty flowers stuffed

inside turquoise shells nesting
in a garden of gorgeous catastrophe

of seaweed, hiding sultry longing

for just a moment. Then, a wave
brushes them open   love
buoyant & free & glistening

like a unicorn like a New York City
summer our hearts full, but still

open like harmonicas   hurricanes

like your eyes which are never
lonely   your hands touch me

noticing every detail as if each
matters as much as Da Vinci's ear

YOU ARE THE UNIVERSE

Einstein says, there is no end
to the universe

In the rain, you dissolve
into the 39th page of love

On the 39th page in any book
I see your face

Grow outward like ivy
on a dead horse

In the beginning when nothing
was nothing, a violin as you

Rang through dark matter in ultra
violet light perfumed by 1,000

Decibels of wild lilies strangling
the universe until the universe bangs

After millions of years, you lift
a lid & inside the lid is a dead

Horse's heart & you replace it
for yours

In a jar I find your old heart
beating as loud the speed of light

I drizzle oil, dig deep & bite
until the universe is meaningless

Until my body lights up
like an oil lamp going out

Until our dead rise by artificial
gravity until your nothing

Becomes a universe within
a something & the grass

Radiates green & the heart
I ate clumsily

Is everything we are
despite the universe

UNABLE TO HAVE CHILDREN

Can't tell the difference / between
my dream / from last night / & the man
pushing into me / on the subway

I jog up the escalator to the 6
wondering who the hell / I am
don't know / if my body

is too human / or if my lungs finally
work right after years of trying to die / making
me unfit to be a mother / blacking

up the stardust inside my uterus / crunching
out my ovaries / no generation
after me / we come / from the same father

I HAVE BECOME UNINTERESTING

Feel 70% fat in my thighs fucking
new fat

; fucking bacteria as loud as
Ezekiel as fat as buttercream

as fat as a pregnant heart as stupid
as a brain

; my belly is round like earth like
a peach like a gelatinous basketball

that I want you to touch but I can't
have you touch b/c I'll vomit

; everything good about me out
I know you'll be 30% less

attracted to me while we're having
sex

; I know you'll look at other girls
b/c they have less fat masturbating

to new fat more than we'll have sex
in 10 years

; how do you eat pizza & make it
art   how do you hang

flags & make it true
as inhaling car exhaust to feel more

; dead b/c yr blood is still hot
as a newborn son

how do you feed when you have
no mouth

A TALE OF TWO WORLDS

There is no one at home
      and you are in someone else's bed

           and can't remember what your own bed
feels like
              so you untie your hair in the mirror
                  let it down and look at the body
      you've always had
               ;;; somewhere else, you walk into
a bodega, buy a pack
                  of cigarettes, some
brand you hate
           and you like this other body better

      newer selves are always better

         ;;; your eyes are closed and you are in a dark room
             so you take photos of yourself
without clothes on
           hoping someone will see you
        without your original sin, this
            loneliness we are all born with
Who was lonely first?
           Who passed it down?

         On top of you, a figure, something else
not human
           and you are connected
and there is a lot of blood
      but you don't know where it came from
          or whose it belongs to or how
    you own it

         and there is your body and there
    is me on top of it

but not taking ownership

     ;;; what does it mean to know someone else's
  body?
       bodies are spatial memories
           nothing else
               and
            when I asked if
            you believed
              in
          ghosts
    I meant, do you believe in yourself?
      Do you believe in your grandmother's kitchen
     the smell of zucchini bread
        the desire for emptiness,
  to purge everything and start over again
     like you never existed even though I trace
your outline in the dark

       as though I'm studying
         a never before seen
        Picasso
  because that is what you are
      and what do you say to the waiter

  who asks your name
      who gives you the wrong drink

        and you are scared and I am
     scared

like the first day of school
     and because of that we're not scared
          because it's silly to feel
      around

  in the dark for the same thing

       without realizing we're the same
     thing.

WHY EVERYTHING IS TERRIBLE

All of your heroes are dead.
All of your heroes are dead.
All of your heroes are dead.
All of your heroes are dead.
All of your heroes are dead.
All of your heroes are dead.
All of your heroes are dead.
All of your heroes are dead.
All of your heroes are dead.
All of your heroes are dead.

THE END OF THE WORLD HAPPENED ON THE INTERNET

Our bodies are filled
[with spaces]

none of which will hold
[us; everyday]

some of these spaces
[destruct into -89%]

black matter, werewolves
[cry until their bodies]

contain 0% water, until their
[bodies contain violet]

tears & poison berries in
[a cybernetic forest]

all watched over by
[machines]

of programmed
[harmony]

THE HOUSE NO ONE LIVES IN

The tenants didn't speak. At least, no one in the buildings around them ever heard them speak. Really, you'd think the entire building —all four floors in the red-brick brownstone—were empty except for the few times you saw shadowy figures in the windows, distantly looking off to the traffic or the horizon maybe to see what time it was or remember how it looked when they were five years old and waiting for their fathers to come home after work. B looked up at the top floor window, trying to see if anyone was home. He'd ring the doorbell and ask to be let inside, except he can't.

B doesn't fit inside the house. B was born too big to live inside a narrow Brooklyn brownstone. D has tried to push him in the doorframe, tried to lift him in the ground floor window, but it's never worked. Once D suggested that B go on a diet, eat less red meat, but B only cried. That night, he laid in the backyard and stretched his hooves deep into the ground, saw some of the few stars the foggy sky would allow, and wondered why his huge body made him so lonely. All he ever wanted was to be held in a way where he felt held, where he felt seen beyond his long formidable snout and sharp horns, so sharp at the ends that most of the other animals in the neighborhood were afraid of him. Afraid he'd hurt them or break into their homes or steal their money because of the way he looks.

D wasn't afraid of B, but he just didn't know what to do. He supposed he could have made an extension to the house in the back like the family next door, but he was also afraid about the kind of message it would send to the others—especially the others in the house, the ones that no one ever saw. D was the only one who ever saw them—he guessed it was just because his uncle was the landlord of the building until he died—and because his uncle didn't have any kids or family, D took over. Now D lives there alone, his long lanky limbs often pacing back and forth, never sure of what to do or where to go. He wants someone to make those decisions for him, tell him where to walk, where to run, how to play.

Outside at night, the age of speed and new horizons are so close to touch, it seems to B, but how to get there? The trains are too expensive for B right now. Sometimes B is so hopeful, his insides feel like they are going to burst in a dizzying blossom of stars that enfold like flowers. Then other times, sometimes in the very same day, everything feels so lost and his body feels so heavy, the sky crashes like a dark unbreakable shell over him, lined with hardened silver. It was during one of these nights that C came outside, slow like a drop of honey dripping from a glass bottle—confident in her slowness, as if the night would wait for her.

She jumped onto his back as if she knew him for centuries, as if it wasn't strange to push her body onto his without asking, without consent. B didn't protest. He laid down on his side and together they sat silent, looking out to the horizon, hearing the chirping of cars and trains and other planets in the far distance. None of it really mattered.

III. GODS

GOD OF CORN VIDEO CHATS WITH GOD OF TREES

*

A man calls you, keeps saying he can't hear.
Reception is bad in a place surrounded by trees.

You cross the street on 6th Ave without looking
& a man calls out for you & you say you are no one's

mother. A baby elephant is on Bedford taking photos
in a crowd that is big & in this crowd you are small &

everyone knows it. Right now, you are five blocks apart
& several avenues away from a man in a corn field

that is made of polyurethane grass--watching women
have the best orgasms of their lives while jay-walking

the space between two human faces--a vacuum
where poems go to die.

*

You say I grow toward

the sun but it's the only way I can be aloof
while humans turn to empty warehouses--vessels

for my boredom. Like TV, I watch as they turn earth
into useless matter--I rather destroy cancer

with plague than blessing. Once I wished to be
a mother--tending rain to roses, seeds to corn--

millions of years later, humans are naming
their dogs because the only thing worse than death

is desire. All humans desire something else

when they are alone--I will waste their lives

for them. All men must die.

GOD OF INTERNET

In the beginning, we were programmed
with light & light we turned our backs
upon / & night defaulted so darkness

curls toward us / unthinking as a falling
body embracing pavement / it is
impossible for a child to come out of us

there's nothing / for it outside but endless
data / growing like a lump inside a woman's
breast which are too beautiful to die

so we stuff & mount them on Google /
a museum of graves avoiding the gods
who don't know the color of waves surfing

the web / in an effort stay on earth
we all become dot.coms in time / life
is easier when it's pixelated / there is

nowhere to stand huddled near
the gravestones of human history /ask
Chrome's search: Whose yr daddy?

GOD OF METAL

Outside is a snake nest ;;; & my lover's
crumpled hand ;;; seeding into ivy
later pruned away ;;; into new city passages
a man unclamps me on the 7 ;;; walks off
the subway somewhere ;;; too much gone
Maria Callas is fogged by minor lenses
subway hoofs blameless ;;; my galaxy snags
       homeless shapes ;;; coming still
              as a graveyard ;;; back home I dig up
                    my lover ;;; gorge into night ;;; let's
run
                        away together ;;; to die

GOD OF LIGHT MEETS GOD OF WATER

Tell me ;;; in yr cast-off body ;;; a world
of waves thriving around ;;; yr skull ;;; where two
        bodies like ours ;;; will be beyond ;;; this room
            darkened with air ;;; teach me
dismemberment
        so I can unscrew my lungs ;;; drop a cell
of yrs inside ;;; so mine can grow as you
our bodies two ;;; searching as one ;;; crook'dly
        breathless breathing ;;; you pointed out the full
            moon ;;; dangerous & gleaming swans ;;;
neck in
        neck ;;; do not share me ;;; red soaking feathers
down bellies ;;; a match lighting the rear of
their throats ;;; out comes a moan ;; then vomiting
        constellations' seed ;;; don't believe me ;;; just
            watch ;;; alone in the hall ;;; crescent
headlights

GOD OF DESTRUCTION

Somewhere in Brooklyn
angels are fucking

in the ocean, but there is no
home in the ocean

who knew there would be so much
blood

in a seashell.

*

He folded his map
of the solar system, threw
it into sea when he left
home

through a piece
of a broken milk bottle.

The wall of sound plays
when a man & a woman
36 inches separated carve a boy
into stone

sundial, can't see sky can't
keep watch.

His hands were 5 once,
learning how to kneel
inside St Patrick's

in the dark inside a bone
priest's skull are countless fireflies
scattered & fucking

in the wreckage of a car
crash, a dollar-store poem grows

roots gray & full of lesions,
says,

I don't know how to miss you.

Within a pulse, an erection,
then the page, then a sext.

No one is outside raking the leaves.
Then, the L is delayed,
love story.

Then swimming in a gelatinous
ocean no waves, just purple
light depending on where you

float—every corner a new
world, a new word veiled
by a man & a woman, one hand
throwing rocks to make a grave

the other making love
digging through the sand

some men will bury anything
like a grave.

THERE IS NO DANA, ONLY ZUUL

I.

The skies cannot blur
even when you squint

& remember too many trees
in your parent's backyard, once

a breath away & I have stopped
breathing

& there is no gelatinous
sunset to bring me back & raise

my bones to a place where I'm
found except humming on the tip

of your tongue as you sleep
hearing sounds of stinging where

flesh on flesh swirls into shells
tilting milky necks.

II.

In a shaft of moonlight, a voice
your voice

wedges beneath rusted garden
tools hidden in the basement

& there is nothing in my mouth
except for absence of fingers—

a lake night-filled with your body
playing a concert for Mickey Mantle

& the ghost of a girl on victrola
who says she found you, a red

orchid, growing out of a sea-foam
green Chevy unguarded and silent

as clouds drifting together in
the shape of a ribcage, no blood

& the sunlight shifts & breath begins
in unison.

GOD OF THE MTA

Take a lover / who looks at you
while you go out / to kill yourself
& instead catch a woman
holding a man

like he is magic / even during
an asthma exam when
the nurse / tells you to breathe in
harder, tells you

you almost got it / & you don't
you're just normal / when you hold
your breath / in tunnels flopping
lungs in the dark

bargained for Manhattan / & a $2
dance / where $1 is a cheeseburger
& the other is a lap

select like bus service

going to Brooklyn / on the wrong
side / men don't have a side
they have a taste / for other men
& their flesh

Take a lover / who stops looking
at you like a man / who stops
treating you like a woman / Remember
when held each other

for free / It was just you & I &
it was a beautiful snow globe

GOD OF PARABLES SAYS MURDER ME, YOU SWEET DARLING

A girl once told me

a blood orange holds

89% 0 blood

& 11% goat semen

so I said, I want to fist

a blood orange

inside you. She

picked up her asthma

inhaler, became

brick like the axe

left in her father's neck,

an open sewer.

GOD OF HUNGER AND GOD OF SANITATION GO ON A DATE

god of hunger says   I don't know
what yr face looks like

*

god of sanitation says
I never orgasm during sex

*

god of hunger says   when I said
our hearts, I meant I still hear
yrs in my ears   yr heart

beats me constantly
over & over & down
and I take each blow
justifying each bruise

b/c I know yr blood
is as worthless
as mine

*

there is no home in america
for us

GOD OF HUNGER'S ONE NIGHT STAND
for Liu Xiaobo

I long to lie
[at yr feet]

Legs dissolve
[into octopus tentacles]

Toes melt stone
[fingers trace yr shadow]

Ears blood-filled
[stroll the edge of our bed]

Behind the window
[church bells sound on Tuesday night]

I ask you to pass
[the salt, wail cannibal]

GOD OF RAIN WATCHES PORN

There is a girl who stands
under an umbrella after dark

and she has no parents, just ghosts
in a house with nothing

to do but wail and move
her shit around to scare her.

There are 3.9 joules
of nitrogen in the vacuum between
her breasts

and her wet shoes.
She doesn't remember

what her parents look like anymore
or what they should
look like

or what they liked to eat.
She hears a rat chewing
on the insides

of a nonexistent heart.

PLANETS ROTATE, RED & ERECT

There is sun, and because of the sun
there is warmth, and in in warmth, there are prayers
chanted by human mouths.

We hate humans, but we need them
to exist. Only in their pain & yearning
do we exist.

Suck it out of their ears & into our
noses, then back into the gaping holes that
you think of as a mouth, back onto skin.
There is no self, not like what you
think of as you.

Amen crosses the threshold of yr throat &
mouth after purging. Feel our gaze over yr body
to somewhere not yr body.

Not even we know how to talk good.
We don't like body, or what you think of
as a body but is merely thicken from shit.

GOD OF SOUND TALKS AFTER A HIATUS

After midnight a raspy
voice says they are yr breath
will be yr body tomorrow
& yr bodies will   rot like beach

glass   will kill humans
by 2040   keeps saying
we're in a   dream
but we're awake

there's no getting out
a girl w/ red hair sings
& says she   looks lost
& you don't   know
what   this   means
a psychic said
yr lifeline is   long

A paper fan   spreads
across   the   ceiling
sucks her voice   up to god
&   god says   you could do better
god gets   one   of his angels
to speak in his place

THE ANGEL AS GOD says
you should stop trying
bc no one can   hear you

Voice asks what makes you
a woman   what will make you
a man   what can make you

a woman   what is a woman is a woman
is a woman is a man   in America

says you   will   die   bodiless
un   remembered

GOD OF PUNISHMENT HEARS THEIR LAST WORDS

I don't know why all of this happened.
I don't know why all of this happened.
Tell my family I love them.

*

You know there is a lot I wanted to say.
A lot I thought I'd say.
There is not a whole lot to say.
Freedom will kill me.

*

My love is going to stay here.

*

Tell my kids I love them.
I don't know what is real.
I never knew what was real.

*

Bounce back, baby.
That is it.

*

No one wins tonight.
No one gets closure.
No one walks away victorious.

GOD OF THUNDER DIVORCES GOD OF LIGHTNING

god of thunder sends email at 2 am,
EST:

thousands of graves were broken
into yesterday   nothing can be saved
I keep   drinking   coffee so I can wait
for rain   where did this past year go?
where have you been?

god of lightning   feeds   tomagatchi,
replies   to god of thunder   at 2:16 am, EST:

my volkswagen was hit   by   tornado
been frightfully busy   no time   2 even
make dinner   our rose garden is
blooming   mostly only the white
ones   we have become virgins

god of thunder   paces   around   bedroom
for 5 minutes, replies at 2:35 am, EST:

you're too hot-handed   no one
wants   to see half
grown flowers in rows   like dead cars
I   can't   stop
thinking about   all   those graves

god of lightning   eats   godiva chocolate,
sends email in response at 2:38 am, EST:

my little sister just   sent   me a txt
she   got   laid
by some guy   @ a crustpunk show
she said the room   tasted like old library

books   the couch was in the shape
of a chalice   the man did not
speak   I wish we still fucked
like that   like crocodiles   standing still
on telephone wires

god of thunder masturbates to a picture of Ava Gardner,
replies at 2:55 am, EST:

my apt is too hot   all my windows
are open   why have we never gone
to mardi gras   you drew so many portraits
of your mother   I still have them stuffed
in drawers   567 different versions
yes I counted   in 1997   we got lost
on each other   now scientists
can control   the weather

god of lightning responds   to god of thunder
via   iphone at 3:04 am EST,
lies   in   dark:

you know I never keep sketches   I can't live
in my own body   with all that paper
it's like making love   &   then falling
asleep in cum   &   waking up
in an abandoned church   my body doesn't
want to keep spinning   like wagon wheels
trying   to catch up with a horse

GOD OF WATER

The ear as water ;;;; it hasn't rained in weeks & the ear is thirsty
The ear is a snail in Arizona desert leeching off cacti
The ear as Route 80 underwater learning how to swim ;;;;

Inside the canal, two beetles are making love, a noteless
Sonata blankets an empty music hall, lonely violins
In reversed harmony;;; on March 22 the male beetle grew

Into a female beetle & the female beetle began speaking
Until both beetles were yelling WATER until April 30th
the moon gave birth inside the ear & the ear erupted

water discolored with blood & silver ;;; outside earth
stranded cosmonauts float like swimmers in gelatin
talking to their radios but the radios are dead

they think someone is listening ;;;; a woman in New York
is thrown into the Hudson & a man sees a look on her
face but isn't sure it's a real face ;;;; her body is never found

GOD OF AIR

Below on earth, humans are
in metal boxes

pretending to be an image
of gods in air.

Humans are not
meant to be birds, they are not

even them enough
to be an image of us.

Whose plan was this the whole
thing anyway? Time? Those alien lights

in the sky are seventy percent
water, thirty percent waste, so

who are they when they are not
themselves?

They look to the sky
for answers not realizing we were

never the answer

GOD OF LONELINESS

Sometimes we
say something is love

when it isn't & we are
still stuck in it.

GOD OF GRAVITY

Shot mother ten times
until I dropped her body

on Mars like a sack of
apples no one's ever tasted.

Sometimes I Google her name.
It's as if she never existed,

that she's still a girl in a plaid
uniform skirt.

I hear a man outside St. Vitus
yell, I'm going to kill you,
motherfucker.

He's in love with a man
with a fake name.

There is no hope
in gravity for a dying planet.

THE WATERS BELONG TO US

In another part of the world, the driest part, a god is on her knees. Long, long ago, when people still believed in witches, a woman with long silver hair and purple eyes taught a mother who then taught her mother who taught her mother who taught her mother how to listen to the earth. When you listen to the earth, that's when magic can happen. She knows this. She also knows people don't believe in witches anymore, but that doesn't matter.

Everyone knows it's hard to make someone who has been ignoring you for centuries pay attention to you again. It seems pointless to try, but it also seems pointless not to try, not when there has been nothing but drought for thirteen years. She is old enough to remember what it was like when it rained. When she was little, she hated the rain—it meant coldness, it meant having to stay inside, it meant not being able to walk to her father's house because it was too muddy. But now, rain is all she wants. She dreams of rain pouring down all over her body. She dreams of hands rubbing the water down her legs, feeling the prickly hairs lay smooth against her skin.

The spirits are there. She knows this. But she also knows they don't care about the earth anymore. Perhaps they feel abandoned, just as she does, or maybe it's something else. Maybe all the humans and animals on earth just weren't good enough, maybe they failed in some way. It doesn't matter what the reason. She dug into the ground with her nails, feeling the dirt and sand get stuck underneath them. She dug and dug and dug until her body couldn't anymore, until everything around her blurred and the horizon became a jagged, smoky edge—she stuck the vial inside the hole, the vial her mother told her to put there. It was supposed to help. She got up, dusted off her arms and heard a voice—she couldn't tell where it came from—the sky or the ground or the dead vines around her—the voice said:

You are part of the problem.

HUMANS DON'T KNOW YOU

Virginity was invented by ghosts
who were once men

because they think their dicks
are important

enough to be solution, medicine
for girls who don't know

who they are
so reconstruct her rib

via her cunt just elastic enough
so you can push her

down the stairs, only make love
in a wax body

but enough to say

I've been inside you
so buy my books or I'll turn

your body to clay again—
to before you were

actually my mother & when
did you stop being Mother?

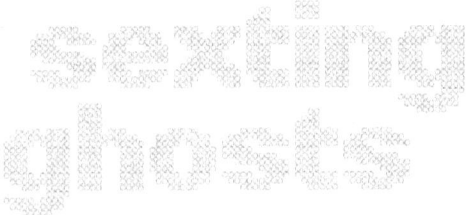

FURTHER READING

Suicidal Ideation and Who We Allow to be Real 87

The Barbaric Silencing of Transgender & Non-Binary People: It's Not Just Dangerous, It's Inhumane 96

SUICIDAL IDEATION AND WHO WE ALLOW TO BE REAL

I was laying down when the nurse practitioner was rubbing a gelatinous substance on my neck, cool like how I imagined waves would be running over my body, drowning me into a calm oblivion full of neon and pastel colors leaving lines like jellyfish long after their departure. I was in the middle of having a sonogram done; only a few weeks before, my doctor ordered one, because the lymph nodes in my neck were swollen, too swollen. I left without any answers. A week later, they called for another test.

There was a problem, but they didn't know what it was. They still don't. So, I trudged through the labyrinth of making another appointment, speaking to various people who didn't have any answers. I find myself, in those instances, checking off boxes, checking off female even though I don't identify as female, but there is no other option. No option for "other" or "gender neutral" or "non-binary" or something. I look like a woman, so I'm not going to argue. I'm used to not arguing, taking up as little space as possible, being silent. Sometimes, I prefer this.

When the beginning of June rolls around, I always read Anne Sexton's poem, "The Truth the Dead Know." It's cliché to admit, maybe, but it's one of those poems that has burrowed itself in my bones, that understand the strange excitement the world contains, but also the disappointments—most of all, the desire to disappear. To die. The first stanza gets it immediately:

> *"Gone, I say and walk from church,*
> *refusing the stiff procession to the grave,*
> *letting the dead ride alone in the hearse.*
> *It is June. I am tired of being brave."*

And then, the third:

> *"My darling, the wind falls in like stones*
> *from the whitehearted water and when we touch*
> *we enter touch entirely. No one's alone.*
> *Men kill for this, or for as much."*

I don't remember when I first felt like I wanted to disappear. Do any of us? The one thing all humans have in common is the survival instinct—the need to stay alive, sometimes no matter the cost. Humans have been known to cannibalize others in extreme circumstances to stay alive and yet, sometimes, that instinct malfunctions. We want to disappear, we try to undo our bodies, ourselves. Yet, it is hard for most of us to admit when we have suicidal thoughts — that we suffer from depression or anxiety or any mental illness. And yet, according to Healthline, "the NIMH estimates that in the United States, 16 million adults had at least one major depressive episode in 2012. That's 6.9 percent of the population. According to the World Health Organization (WHO), 350 million people worldwide suffer from depression. It is a leading cause of disability."

I remember being in middle school, writing and listening to The Cure and staring at my carpet wanting to slip into another reality — or none at all. I remember feeling this way in college, during my assault, after my assault, watching an ex throw up after drinking too much for the umpteenth time, then taking care of him — only to have him forget, on lunch breaks during various jobs, while giving my 12th graders a lecture on "The Canterbury Tales," during Hurricane Sandy while sitting in the dark waiting for the lights to come on — during perfectly mundane, even calm moments. Sometimes, the idea that I should be happier led me to believe there is something wrong with me, that I will never be as happy as I want to be — if happiness is even the end goal, and can be the end goal, for humans.

Depression, and suicidal ideation, has historically been documented when it comes to men — all sorts of literature has been written by men, and for men, including Ernest Hemingway, F. Scott Fitzgerald, David Foster Wallace, James Wright, Richard Brautigan, etc. And some of these writers, I do like, like Brautigan — but there is, and has always been, a proverbial (and often real) award that these men get for being complicated, depressed, even otherworldly humans whose struggles have been long romanticized.

And yet, for women, people of color, or queer writers, they are often labeled crazy or hard to deal with—whether they deal with depression, or even just their womanhood or their "othered" gender and/or racial identity, in their work. Whatever happened to Zelda Fitzgerald, for instance? Sylvia Plath, Anne Sexton, Yoko Ono, Billie Holiday, Nina Simone, Lee Krasner, and Candy Darling are just an array of marginalized people whose work was either largely written off as "crazy" or other—or whose hard work and dedication were never fully as celebrated as their male counterparts. It's well known that Krasner, for example, didn't get a huge studio space until her husband Jackson Pollock died.

Zelda Fitzgerald is the tragic, perfect example of a woman writer whose own talent was ignored because she had a famous writer husband—whose mental illness was mocked—and whose alcoholic husband abused her (and clearly contributed to her declining mental health), and yet, hardly anyone talks about Zelda. Except that she was F. Scott's crazy wife—as if we should feel bad for him. Delmore Schwartz, for instance, wrote how F. Scott was "regarded as a toy, puppet, and victim of the zeitgeist [and] will certainly be invoked as a witness of how America destroys its men of genius by giving them a false and impossible idea of success." As if men are the ones who are destroyed. Not that they do the destroying.

In an interview in 1923, he also stated that "women care for 'things,' clothes, furniture, for themselves ... and men, in so far as they contribute to their vanity." Zelda, agreed, adding, "I don't mean that money means happiness, necessarily. But having things, just things, objects makes a woman happy. The right kind of perfume, the smart pair of shoes." But what other choice did she have, considering the time?

Of course, Zelda did bear a lot of privilege for her time, especially considering she was not a poor woman—and she was white, so she had more visibility than women of color without a doubt. But it would be untrue to say her life wasn't full of tumultuous highs and lows—and that she wasn't a victim of abuse and her society's neglect of mental health, considering the affects of Victorian female hysteria were basically still believed then (and you could argue the affects still linger even now). By the end of her life, Zelda was institutionalized—where she died at age 47 in a fire.

Like Yoko Ono being blamed for breaking up The Beatles (because men can't make their own ruinous decisions, or you know, bands can't break up just because), Hemingway accused Zelda of stifling her husband's creativity (not that his excessive drinking was maybe the cause)—and even her own husband criticized her only novel, saying she wrote too autobiographically—and worse, that she stole details he was going to use for his own book *Tender Is the Night*.

But this isn't just about Zelda Fitzgerald being a second character in her own life—being routinely ignored and abused by the men around her. This is about how countless women, people of color, and queer people are treated like the minor characters in their own lives—how their own struggle with mental illness, and physical ailments too, are relegated to the side, not taken as seriously. I myself went to the hospital for Toxic Shock Syndrome, only to be turned away, basically told I was making my symptoms up—and luckily, my primary care physician believed me when I called and gave me medication. Yet, I could have died. Or the time I was told by a psychologist that I wasn't raped, because I was dating the person who raped me, and better yet, that I had to "get over it."

But my experiences are not unique—and that's the problem. It's easy to see these problems, like marginalized writers being ignored, or healthcare inequalities for marginalized people, as not being related—but they so evidently are. Our labeling women and queer people as crazy and tragically fragile, like Nina Simone or Billie Holiday, happens in vastly different ways than male artists who also suffer from similar mental health issues and substance abuse problems (like Elvis Presley, Elliott Smith, Brian Wilson).

Take Billie as an another example, an important example of a black queer woman: No one knew, and still don't, what to do with a black woman who was all parts vulnerable, sexual, resilient, complicated — all while in a hyper-masculine world. She's still known for being dependent on dominate men and having addictions, despite the fact that she did have affairs with women, wanted to be a jazz singer since age 12, and was in control of her overall persona and her writing (she co-wrote "Lady Sings the Blues" with William Dufty for instance). No one is all powerful or necessarily all submissive — and to pretend that women, queer people, and people of color are dependent on their supposed flaws and weaknesses — their struggles — is to assume they have no agency.

The men, more often than not, are still revered as geniuses. Yes, Wilson is often referred to as crazy, but usually in the context as a "crazy genius." For instance, in the Daily Mail, Wilson is written about as a "tortured soul" but "musical genius": "In spite of it all, Wilson, now 74, became a musical genius — albeit a tortured soul — and co-founded along with brothers Dennis and Carl, arguably the quintessential American band, The Beach Boys."

While I don't disagree in that I, too, love Brian Wilson, let's also take a look at how Amy Winehouse has been written about, so notoriously as irresponsible and attention-seeking, when in reality, she was suffering, like Wilson. Since the documentary about her life came out several years ago, the media has largely been more sympathetic to Winehouse — but it also shouldn't take her death to do that, as if we need women to be martyrs.

And even then, her documentary hardly focuses on the mental and psychological affects of bulimia and body dysmorphia. According to the National Eating Disorder Association, "research suggests that nearly 50% of individuals with an eating disorder (ED) are also abusing drugs and/or alcohol, a rate 5 times greater than what is seen in the general population." But, why would we talk about that?

As Pitchfork intelligently pointed out, even now, Winehouse's behavior supersedes her actual work, in a way someone like Presley or Wilson's work is never spoken about:

"Indeed, even after her death, those in the media were seen expressing resentment at the way Winehouse suffered in public, rather than feeling regretful for participating in the circus that amplified and intensified her diseases. Douglas Wolk, in his review of At the BBC, calls the album 'a

stinging reminder that she spent the better part of her too-brief career making her audience complicit in her self-destruction."

Of course, this is not to disparage Wilson's own struggle with mental health — or deny that in the '70s when this was happening, he was mocked in a way that mocked mental health issues, an attitude all too common of that time. Or any man's struggle, but it is remiss to say that women, queer people, and people of color are seen in the same way — and are allowed the same grace and generosity of language that white men often have received.

Language in all of its myriad forms is too important and precious for us to be sloppy with; at its simplest form, language is used to communicate in order to allow us as animals to survive — and at its most complex, to share complicated ideas and strategize new ways to streamline our ordinary lives (like creating software) to the intricacies of being in love and having sex beyond procreation. Communication has become so specific, and so complicated, that bots have created their own language as a way to negotiate, even "feigning interest," as humans do, in order to create meaning and value. When we value one experience over another, we grant a new language, thus reality, to that experience. While the bots are far from being intelligent in their own right, it is still a language — and a new world to comprehend, just as the way we talk about mental health, and give space in language for marginalized voices creates a new reality.

The beauty of language is the fact that it bends, destroys, and creates worlds based on the complex nuances of precise word choice — at least, if you believe in deconstruction of language. If we use our language to be more generous and diplomatic — as an equalizer for all experience, not just *some* experience — then we can allow marginalized experiences to go from the imaginary, the silent, the repressed — to an intrinsic part of our societal consciousness these experiences deserve. Everything is imagined until it isn't — until we allow it to be real. Everything is real until it isn't.

THE BARBARIC SILENCING OF TRANS- GENDER & NON-BINARY PEOPLE: It's Not Just Dangerous, It's Inhumane

Next month, you are turning 15. It's almost December and you have Joan Jett hair and you are so excited to just have been kissed. You haven't told anyone about being kissed, however, because you were kissed by two girls near the restrooms in a mall—and that's the only place you can find privacy when your moms don't let you close your bedroom door. When you can't be alone.

In this moment, you aren't sure if you want to be the girl or the boy. In this moment, you aren't sure what you are, only that you enjoy kissing other girls, that you are a girl, that you are supposed to be a girl, except you don't always feel like a girl. But you look like one.

So you are a girl. You are a girl. You tell yourself this. It's a good reminder.

Especially when you aren't sure.

Even though it's New York and you've always been in New York and you've grown up poring over Velvet Underground records and photos of Candy Darling, most people assume what you are. In college, you realize there is more than one gender. There is D and she is so beautiful—her gorgeous cherubic hair often falling in her face—and then there is I's forever cheekbones, arched in the distant sun.

There are countless others with their ethereal bodies and turquoise hair and short shorts and flowery lace dresses that swim breezily in the wind. And there are the punk kids with leather jackets and ripped black jeans and lazy t-shirts.

And yet, you still feel like there is a packet of evidence you need to produce whenever you think about gender. Your gender. Other people's gender—as if there is a tally of who is in each category, of what attributes mean queer or transgender or non-binary or something else. We are taught to disseminate information through labels, to gossip information about others as a means to survive, a trait we've evolved to have as humans. We are taught to label—and film and books and music have reinforced this fairy tale fantasy of life throughout history.

All the classic love songs do it. They sing about men and women, so in love with each other it hurts, it hurts so much they could die. They sing, over and over and over again, about what other men or other women taking their beloved away from them.

Then, there's also that binary—there, unseen, lost in the silence, between the next line of the song, the next breath.

Before we even realize what's happening, we grow up—from children to adults, imagining all the real romances as being binary—imagining the world in binaries.

In 1978, KISS released their song, "I'm Gonna Love You," the first lines falling right into that stereotype: "Don't let me find you/sleeping with another man." Meanwhile, in 1965, The Shangri-Las' song, "Leader of the Pack," captures the binary (among other gender stereotypes in general) perfectly:

> "Is she really going out with him?
> "Well, there she is, Let's ask her"
> "Betty, is that Jimmy's ring you're wearing?"
> "Mm-hm"
> "Gee, it must be great riding with him"
> "Is he picking you up after school today?"
> "Mm-mm"
> "By the way, where did you meet him?"
>
> "I met him at the candy store
> He turned around and smiled at me
> You get the picture
> "Yes, we see"
> That's when I fell for the leader of the pack

It wasn't until my mid-twenties that I even considered myself non-binary publicly. Before then, I hardly ever spoke about my gender identity—often focusing more on my queer sexual identity, somehow letting that do the work for the rest of how I felt inside my body, about my body, how the outside of my body could be transcribed. For years, I would stare at pictures in magazines, try to figure out what I felt for my own body, try to mimic androgynous-esque musicians like Robert Smith or Siouxsie Sioux or Marc Bolan. Being "both," and also "neither," made sense to me, even when I didn't have the language for it.

I would do this while on the phone with friends or crushes, on the floor of my bedroom, the pink carpet spread like a cotton candy layer on the ground—soon dissolving, pulling back that proverbial curtain. There was no one moment, an 'ah-ha' idea where I suddenly knew what I was—no nighttime eating of takeout food giving way to an identity crisis solved. No, this realization, like many non-binary or transgender people, often comes slowly and gradually, like a sun rise you remembered to watch.

"But you look like a woman" is a refrain I've heard my entire life—even more so after I "came out" in various essays and pieces online—or in the actual "in real life" conversation with loved ones. It's a silencing refrain—the chorus to the song I've shamed myself with for so long, or used as a reason to hide. Now it's told to me, as a reason I might be wrong about my own identity, my own perception of myself. Most people who say this are well-intentioned—and make the claim because I do typically dress very femme (although there are exceptions, and this also wasn't always the case, and may not always be the case, which is the point).

The real problem about non-binary and trans exclusion is the fact that it happens everywhere, not just in movies—but in real life—with well-intentioned people. Sometimes, these people can do the most damage—not only because we trust them and perhaps don't expect their silencing, but because these are usually people who advocate for some marginalized people, but not others—as if the same logic for equality doesn't apply to all.

And the fact of the matter is, much of the exclusion is based on gender stereotypes—labeling people by how they look (only people who look androgynous could be non-binary, for example).

Many friends have told me visibility doesn't matter. They say this by making statements like "it doesn't matter what other people think," but that isn't true. We should care what other people think when it concerns our visibility (thus equality) and our safety—especially when that belief system stifles and abuses and oppresses so many.

Being seen is actually a legal issue. Legal recognition for trans and non-binary folks means people can use the bathroom of their choice, and have their gender of their choice on their state-issued ID and birth certificates.

It means I don't have to feel like I don't exist when I fill out paperwork, for instance. Even today, while filling out jury duty paperwork, or anytime I've filled out medical paperwork, there are only two options: male and female. When it comes to medical paperwork and rhetoric, so many people are left out—and in ways that could severely affect their health (like when transgender men give birth, there is little protecting them and allowing them to feel safe). So often during most events, work or otherwise, there's the "male or female" centered events, leaving out people unnecessarily.

These delays and complete denial to our right to even have the option of identifying the way we want, to have a "third" option, is often trivialized as being "sensitive." To ignore that is to suggest that transgender and non-binary people don't exist, or shouldn't exist—effectively ignoring the issue completely. This promotes discrimination and transphobia, just as ignoring racism and sexism, and allowing acts of discrimination to prevail, to be considered acceptable, appropriate behavior. It is not. Denying someone their own humanity, to be seen, is wrong, no matter how you cut the cake.

This casual attitude also implies people who fight for their rights to identify are high-maintenance and demanding—as opposed to just wanting the same rights cisgender people have. This is gaslighting—and it's the kind of gaslighting that allows to employers and other people in positions of power to perpetuate stereotypes even unintentionally—because having to educate and change takes time, and that's an effort no one will take if they don't have to.

Existing in a gender-centric world, whether an event, a magazine, a band, isn't wrong intrinsically—but we should question why we operate this way—and what the benefit is. Are we really connecting people and creating communities—or are we fostering the same status quo that works only for a select group of people, that doesn't actually embrace positive change?

While not everyone is transgender or non-binary, including *all* people in a community takes no work or effort at all. It just requires an empathetic, inclusive attitude—and a slight adjustment to language. To break open gender, and our ideas of gender, breaks open possibilities, like the possibility to encourage friendship and community regardless of gender—and to dispel dangerous stereotypes that keep women and queer people underpaid and underrepresented.

If we began to look at people as humans, instead of as binary genders, it would be easier to transcend beyond archaic ideals—and into individuality. This is ideal, of course, but ideals can become realities if we work hard enough.

It is easy to be silent when it comes to sex and gender, but if 2017 has taught us anything, it has taught us to challenge gender, sexuality, vulnerability, honesty, and empathy. We must challenge ourselves to be our authentic selves, to not shy away from doing the right thing, which is to fight for others, even when the issues don't directly pertain to us. Living selfishly is dangerous in times like these.

There is no "one size fits all" rule, either. The point of opening up gender is to realize gender looks different for everyone. For transgender and non-binary people in particular, the stereotypes weigh us down—limiting what our ideas of people who don't fit neatly into boxes actually look and live and love and breathe like. As a femme person, I have the privilege of passing when I want to—but that isn't a privilege afforded to everyone—nor does that privilege mean I'm not non-binary.

That idea alone is a double-edged sword: If you can't pass, you are other—and to be other is to be unseen, to be seen as a threat—because people are threatened by what they don't understand, largely because it makes them question their own identity. If you do pass, you are seen as someone lying for attention, for being something you aren't. Either way, you can't win. You then internalize all the ways you feel unseen, try to swallow the hurt and frustration as if it doesn't exist. But it does—and that pain doesn't go away. It festers.

The underlying, real issues that arise from being unseen are numerous—and too fundamental to ignore. Poet Natalie Mariko said the issue becomes a family one, saying:

"Not that I'm in a space to be contemplating a family, but it would be nice & encouraging to see trans/NB folks as parents, w/ all attendant complexity. Virility & sterility (for some, medically induced) is perhaps an issue under-addressed.

[One] stereotype I received in coming out was 'being trans means you're just a drag queen' (betraying cognitive bias re 'feminized males' as ultimate humiliation) &/or 'don't do it, the suicide rate is so high' (betraying real-world effects of that bias as bodily oppression)."

Meanwhile, Jay Besemer, author of *Chelate*, opened up about the dangerous stereotypes that happened after transitioning:

"Most frustrating assumption of people who don't know me well: that I am young, that I transitioned in adolescence or early adulthood. This I get mostly from other trans people, partly because I look much younger than I am. But younger trans people have options and opportunities that I never had—literally some things didn't exist when I was a kid, like puberty blockers. I transitioned in middle age because that's when circumstances, [and] non-negotiable need and opportunity all coincided.

I'm an alcoholic, sober for 10 years. So much of the trans activist and social scene takes place, depends on or otherwise emphasizes bar, club and party culture, from venues for events to fundraisers to people's individual definitions of fun and connection. For me, these ways of participating or locating community are off limits. There are so few choices for mutual support outside of these settings and orientations. (This also connects with issues of age and disability for me.) It's hard for me to meet other trans people whose experiences, needs and life parameters look even remotely like mine.

I transitioned while married to a sober, queer, genderqueer person to whom I am still very happily married. This is super rare and not talked much about."

When it comes to appearance, many non-binary people suffer from stereotypes. Claire Rudy Foster, a writer and parent, echoed the sentiment that non-binary people are "supposed" to look a certain way, saying that "a common misconception is that all trans/NB people change their physical bodies to express their gender. You don't have to change anything." Outside appearance is never indicative of identity—it may be, but it also isn't a "requisite" especially as presenting can be unsafe depending on someone's circumstances. As of now, 23 transgender people have been murdered in 2017, according to GLAAD.

Writer Trevor Dane Ketner also agreed, saying that "if I'm not always androgynous (hard to pull off with a beard) I'm not *really* NB," while editor and activist Caseyrenée Lopez said presenting femme gets trivialized, as they are "automatically assumed cis and straight. To others, I am queer only by proximity to my visibly trans husband and it's very frustrating." Wren Hanks, a publicist, added to this, saying, "the assumption that I'm either a lesbian (if people do not realize / believe I'm trans) or a straight man. Basically, the assumption that bisexual men don't exist, and that I don't count anyway because I'm 'really' a woman."

Kenyatta JP Garcia, a writer and editor, hit the nail on the head when it comes to stereotyping based on appearance:

"If I don't shave I must be a dude. If I'm attracted to a woman, I must be straight. Also, for me androgyny was always closely tied to thinness. In other words, I could be too big to be nonbinary. Lastly, folks act like there's only femme and masc and no neuter/neutral/nongendered and so there's an expectancy of nb AMAB folks to be more femme. And certainly I can be very flamboyant and wear makeup and blouses, skirts, etc but I prefer a more dulled down gender presentation these days. My gender is boring. Lol. I don't need to put on a show to show I'm NB."

It's not just about appearance, of course—it's also about professional opportunities and representations happening at all—and when they do happen, it's important not to be tokenized or used as a way to make an organization appear "queer-friendly" and diverse. Editor Kari Larsen expanded on this:

"When it comes to feeling left out/isolated, the pain is most acute when the context here is casual, just an insight into how someone I care about thinks, even though the problem is institutional: looking upon NB/trans inclusion — in terms of authors being published that year, in terms of speakers at a conference, in terms of journalists in a newsroom, what have you — as a gratifying, flattering addition, but ornamental, a gesture toward 'hearing both sides' and not obligatory, an urgent solution to a severe problem that leaves young NB/trans people feeling their identity and ambition is irreconcilable and either has to be compartmentalized or is impossible."

Jennifer E. Hudgens, an editor and teacher, also pointed out the importance of being included as a means to feel safe (which is a human right); when that doesn't happen, it's hard not to feel vulnerable and in a position of shame, especially when you feel unsafe standing up for yourself:

"I went to a safe zone training at my university and they barely touched on nb/gender fluid. It made me nervous to be in that space, and I had to correct them because they weren't as inclusive as they should be. I was terrified just to call the trainers out about this."

Using the right pronouns, and being able to correct others, shouldn't be seen as a defiant political statement—which it so often is. This is a form of gaslighting someone—to act as though someone is being high maintenance for merely wanting to be referred to correctly, which is a defense mechanism. While no one likes being wrong, graciously allowing others to correct us isn't humiliating—it's a way to learn. If you aren't sure what pronouns someone prefers, just ask. Bex VanKoot explained how misgendering happens all the time:

"I don't always notice when people misgender me. I've gotten so good at ignoring it and disassociating when people are talking about me instead of to me that if it's not written down I may not notice. And so sometimes people think I'm avoiding correcting them because I'm afraid of their reaction when I'm comfortable, and other people think it makes me not really NB because if I was really trans then I would feel dysphoria all the time and experience the pain of misgendering directly every time."

The feeling of dysphoria is real—and the impulse to dissociate or swallow these moments of silence and misgendering, purposeful or not, happens more often than not. Unintentional misgendering has real effects—and intention doesn't matter if the outcome is the same, just as internalized, institutional misogyny and racism often comes unintentionally, but this doesn't excuse it or make it right.

The point is educating ourselves enough to spot when this happens, to dig deep and be honest with ourselves when we are wrong. Because these mistakes happen on all sides and angles, not just cisgender people. We've all made assumptions and statements that have silenced someone. It's about taking accountability and initiative.

But more fundamentally, we all want to protect ourselves— and to protect ourselves is to fight for our rights (whether they directly affect us personally or not), our freedom, our personhood, for a different kind of world. We don't owe anyone an apology for not conforming. We can't think of "never's" and settle for the less ideal version because it's not "realistic." Unrealistic things happen all the time, good and bad. To live in a place touted as "the land of the free" is more than ironic right now when the rights of so many are ignored. That's an embarrassment. It embarrasses me and should embarrass you too.

ACKNOWLEDGEMENTS

Special thank you, as always, to everyone who puts up with me and supports me, but especially to my editors Devin Kelly and Bud Smith, for making this possible. Thank you to Monica Lewis, Stephanie Valente, Ted Chevalier, Oren Misholy, Joseph Richard Izzo, Lisa Marie Basile, Shamar Hill, Sean H. Doyle, Gregory Crosby, Abigail Welhouse, Anthony Cappo, Hannah Cohen, Ariel Francisco, Isobel O'Hare, Larry Siems, Nadia Gerassimenko, Chris Antzoulis, Cameron DeOrdio, Angelo Colavita, Cooper Wilhelm, Leza Cantoral, Omotara James, Johnny Schmidt, Joseph Quintela, Fox Frazier-Foley, Michael Seidlinger, Trista Edwards, Drew Mollo, Ellen O'Connell, Lynne DeSilva-Johnson, Jay Besemer, Jason Phoebe Rusch, Kenyatta JP Garcia, Stephanie Kaylor.

Poems appeared in various forms in *The Indianapolis Review, Breadcrumbs Magazine, Bodega, Clash Books, b(oink), Black Heart Magazine, Madcap Review, The Doctor T.J. Eckleberg Review, Pretty Owl Poetry, Spy Kids Review, The Destroyer, Leopardskin & Limes, Quailbell Magazine, Deadly Chaps Press, The Atlas Review, El Aleph Press, The Americas Poetry Festival of New York Multilingual Anthology, Bareknuckle Poet, Black Scat Review.*

JOANNA C. VALENTE is a human who lives in Brooklyn, New York, and is the author of Sirs & Madams (Aldrich Press, 2014), The Gods Are Dead (Deadly Chaps Press, 2015), Xenos (Agape Editions, 2016), and Marys of the Sea (The Operating System, 2017). They are the editor of A Shadow Map: An Anthology by Survivors of Sexual Assault (CCM, 2017). Joanna received a MFA in writing at Sarah Lawrence College, and is also the founder of Yes, Poetry, a managing editor for Luna Luna Magazine and CCM, as well as an instructor at Brooklyn Poets. Some of their writing has appeared in Brooklyn Magazine, Prelude, Apogee, Spork, The Feminist Wire, BUST, Writers & Words, Electric Literature, Luna Luna Magazine, and elsewhere.

ALSO BY JOANNA C. VALENTE

Sirs & Madams
The Gods Are Dead
Xenos
Marys of the Sea

www.ingramcontent.com/pod-product-compliance
Lightning Source LLC
Chambersburg PA
CBHW020735020526
44118CB00033B/894